COOKING
FOR SPECIAL DIETS